I Can Read!

READING WITH HELP 2

BEYOND THE DINOSAURS

MONSTERS OF THE AIR AND SEA

D0201773

by Charlotte Lewis Brown
pictures by Phil Wilson

HarperCollins*Publishers*

To Louis W. Mellott,
grandfather and fisherman extraordinaire
—C.L.B.

To my parents, John and Jane Wilson, with love,
and to my high school art teacher,
Bill Applequist, with gratitude
—P.W.

HarperCollins®, ☎®, and I Can Read Book® are trademarks of HarperCollins Publishers.

Library of Congress Cataloging-in-Publication Data
Brown, Charlotte Lewis.
    Beyond the dinosaurs : monsters of the air and sea / written by Charlotte Lewis Brown ; pictures by Phil Wilson.—1st ed.
        p.   cm. — (I can read book)
    ISBN 978-0-06-053056-3 (trade bdg.) — ISBN 978-0-06-053057-0 (lib. bdg.) — ISBN 978-0-06-053058-7 (pbk.)
    1. Reptiles, Fossil—Juvenile literature. 2. Deinosuchus—Pteranodon—Elasmosaurus—Ichthyosaurus—Mosasaurus—
Microraptor—Kronosaurus—Pterodaustro—Hainosaurus—Placodus—Archaeopteryx.
QE861.5 .B76 2007   2007014462
567.9 22   CIP
                                                                                                                                        AC

12 13 LP/WOR 10 9 8 7 6 5 4 3   ❖   First Edition

CONTENTS

Millions of years ago,
and long before there
were people,
dinosaurs were the most
powerful animals that
walked on land.
Dinosaurs ruled the Earth,
but they did not live
in the air or the water.

Other powerful animals
swam in the sea
and flew across the sky.
These creatures
were just as strange and wonderful
as any dinosaur. . . .

PTERANODON

You say it like this:

ter-AN-oh-don

Pteranodon flew on wings

made of skin

that stretched from its body

to the ends of its arms.

A coat of fine hair

kept Pteranodon warm.

Pteranodon lived near the ocean
and flew above the waves
hunting for food.
It caught fish in its long,
thin beak.

DEINOSUCHUS

You say it like this:

Die-no-SUE-kus

Deinosuchus looked
like a modern crocodile,
but it was more than
five times larger.

It was so big,

it could eat dinosaurs.

It waited underwater

until a dinosaur came to drink.

Then Deinosuchus

pulled the dinosaur underwater

and ate it.

ELASMOSAURUS

You say it like this:

eh-LAZZ-mo-SAWR-us

Elasmosaurus was mostly neck.
It had a fat, round body
and a short tail.

Elasmosaurus was not a fast swimmer,
but it was good at catching fish.

When fish swam by,
Elasmosaurus shot out its long,
skinny neck and grabbed one!

ICHTHYOSAURUS

You say it like this:

ICK-thee-oh-SAWR-us

Ichthyosaurus had fins
and a tail, just like a fish.
But it was not a fish.
Ichthyosaurus was a reptile.
Fish can breathe underwater.
Reptiles must breathe air.
Ichthyosaurus would take
a big breath of air,
then dive underwater
to catch fish to eat.

It would swallow the fish whole,
then spit out the bones.

MOSASAURUS

You say it like this:

MOES-ah-SAWR-us

Mosasaurus was built to swim.

It had a thin body and head.

Its tail was long and strong.

Instead of feet, it had flippers.

Mosasaurus swam
by swinging its tail
from side to side.

It steered with its flippers.
Mosasaurus was the fastest swimmer
in the ocean.

HAINOSAURUS

You say it like this:

EN-o-SAWR-us

Hainosaurus had a thin body,
like Mosasaurus.
But Hainosaurus's head
was shaped like an arrow,
and its nose was made of thick bones.
It would swim fast
and ram prey with its bony nose.

PTERODAUSTRO

You say it like this:

ter-o-DAW-stro

Pterodaustro had hundreds
of long, thin teeth.
The teeth made
Pterodaustro's mouth
look like a fine-tooth comb.
Pterodaustro scooped water
into its mouth,
then spit the water
out through its teeth.
The thin teeth trapped
the tiny sea creatures
that Pterodaustro ate.

MICRORAPTOR

You say it like this:

MY-crow-RAP-tor

Microraptor was the dinosaur
that almost flew.
Long feathers grew on
Microraptor's arms and legs
and, unlike other dinosaurs,
it could climb trees.

Microraptor couldn't fly,
but it would jump from a treetop
with its limbs spread wide
and glide gently to the ground.

KRONOSAURUS

You say it like this:

KRONE-oh-SAWR-us

Kronosaurus was a giant
that hunted the ocean for food.
It was longer than a bus.
It had teeth as big as bananas.

Its jaws were bigger

and stronger than

the jaws of Tyrannosaurus rex.

It ate fish, ichthyosaurs,

and even turtles.

Kronosaurus ate anything it wanted!

PLACODUS

You say it like this:

pla-KO-dus

Placodus lived
both on land and in the water.
It used its powerful tail
to swim underwater,
where it ate food
it found in the mud.

When Placodus grew tired,
it crawled out onto land.
It used its short legs
to walk along the shore
until it found a place to rest.

ARCHAEOPTERYX

You say it like this:

ark-ee-OP-ter-icks

Archaeopteryx was the first bird.

It had wings and feathers,

like modern birds.

But unlike modern birds,

it had long claws on its wings.

It also had

a mouth full of sharp teeth.

Modern birds do not have any teeth.

Archaeopteryx means "ancient wing."

Archaeopteryx and the other animals
in this book lived and died
a long time ago.
We know what they looked like
because their bones were saved
in rocks, called fossils.
Scientists study fossils
to learn about these animals.
Sometimes marks of hair,
feathers, or skin are saved.
We are sure that Archaeopteryx
had feathers because their shapes
can be seen in the rock
that surrounds its bones.

Fossils last a long, long time,
and they are found
all over the world.
When we find new fossils,
we learn even more about
the animals that lived long ago!

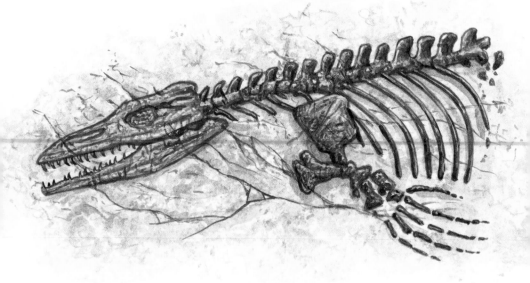